CW00400815

HOW TO WRITE
A BUSINESS PLAN

A practical guidance book for developing
and
writing your business plan

Alessandro Bolasco

ISBN: 9798359209243

Cover design by: Art Painter Library of Congress
Control Number: 2018675309 Printed in the United
States of America

"It is not the most intellectual of the species that survives; it is not the strongest that survives; but the species that survives is the one that is able best to adapt and adjust to the changing environment in which it finds itself."

Leon C. Megginson paraphrasing Charles Darwin's "Origin of Species"

To my son and my wife,
who inspire me to do better every day

CONTENTS

How to Write a Business Plan

Introduction

First thing first: Planning mindset

How to research your market

The competition

Forecasting your sales

What your business plan should include

Expenses and investments

Profit and loss projections

Balance sheet

Cash flow projections

ROI and other important financial ratios

Writing a realistic business plan

About the author

INTRODUCTION

You have a brilliant idea that's been going through your mind for weeks and are now looking to test that idea and, possibly, predict how well it could realistically do.

Or maybe you have already shared your intuition and obtained some positive feedback, perhaps found a co-founder, and are ready to carry out preliminary validation tests.

You may be wondering how you should research your market and build a sensible sales forecast.

Or, at a more advanced stage, you may already have a minimum viable product and a business model, and what you are after now is a well-done business plan.

Whatever phase you are at, this book will help you define your idea and create a reliable business plan to put in front of potential investors, whether these are venture capitalists, business angels, granting bodies, lending institutions, crowdfunding investors, or simply prospective co-founders.

Even where you don't need to raise funds and don't even need a business plan, here you will find extremely useful resources to identify your business proposition and forecast sales over the short and long-term using realistic, practical tools.

The unnecessary has been left out, this is not the place to discuss theories or go into long-winded commentaries. Only concise, to-the-point information, complete with practical examples taken from my activity as a UK-based business consultant.

Having helped entrepreneurs and on-going businesses with the planning and running compliance of their companies, I am delighted to share some of the things I've learnt during my career.

I really hope you will find the content valuable and, equipped with the necessary planning tools, discover your way into the entrepreneurial world.

Alessandro Bolasco

Founder and owner of Bolasco Consulting

FIRST THING, FIRST: PLANNING MINDSET!

Let your creativity point you toward the right direction and your strategic planning guide you to your destination.

Dream, drive, passion, intuition, talent. They are all essential to an entrepreneur's success, but the "let's see how it goes" approach in business is too much of a vague way to go about it. What you need to hit the score is good strategic planning!

- Defining my business model

- Knowing who my target customers are

- By what means I'm going to get my business funded?

- Is it better to start as a self-employed or as a company?

- The key points in my strategy

- A reliable Business Plan

These are only a few of the points you need to work on before embarking on a new business venture.

How many times do we hear things like "Oh, there's a huge demand for that" or "that company is making millions" or "people will always need to buy that".

Reality is there are so many factors at play, both internal and external, that will make your enterprise successful or not, just to mention a few: skills; experience; your business model; the rapport with your business partners, if applicable; location of your business; your employees and contractors; your marketing plan; your knowledge of the competition and of the market; the political conditions in the country where the business is to be based; the international geopolitical stability; the supply industry conditions; how fierce and adaptable your competition is; and the list could go on and on.

Although nobody has a crystal ball, all the before-mentioned factors could and should be analysed and put down into a Business Plan, which will give you a better understanding of your chosen sector and, most of all, grant you a much stronger position in front of any potential investor, be it a VC, business angel, government funding examiner, a bank, or even a friend.

Let your creativity sprout and then assess it against the reality.

Be a realistic dreamer!

And if there are different possible outcomes to a new idea you have, consider those which are more realistic first. You will then be able to build a robust plan and shape it upon different scenarios, the most likely ones of course.

Read on to find out how to assess your idea.

HOW TO RESEARCH YOUR MARKET ONLINE

You have set into a business planning mindset and run a critical analysis of your new proposition.

Now market research, be it! This is a *sine qua non* condition. Before moving any forward, you should carry out proper research to learn about what people are looking for and how this could be converted into sound business.

I am not going to deal with that part of market research delegated to specialised agencies as that is luxury for the big firms only. A new, single-entrepreneur or perhaps two-partner business is likely to have much less resources at their disposal, so diligently carried out online research is the way forward.

Is there a market for your soon-to-be business? Or, more precisely, is there a demand for your product/service? Is it a stable demand or is characterised by seasonality? Is the demand expected to remain the same or to grow or decrease over the next few years? Are there any political /

economical elements in your target region that might affect the demand?

As you go along discovering your potential customer base, you will also find there isn't only one market segment; there are many, and within each one of them you will be able to single out various product/market segments, which means that for each product line there will likely be several market segments.

For example, if you intended to sell shoes to customers of different ages, you might have one segment for sports shoes for customers aged 5-10; one for sports shoes for customers aged 11 over; one for school shoes; one for elegant shoes young adults (not for school); one for elegant shoes for office customers.

Google Keyword Planner

This is one of the most effective tools to find out what users are looking for, how they are looking for it and where they are located.

Let's say you want to start an event planning business in London.

While, clearly, kids party events are rather a different story than wedding events or sports events, the following example will give you a hint as to how to find the prospective market demand in your targeted area.

What is the first thing that you, as someone who is looking for an event planner in London, would do? I would take to Google and start with "Event planners in London" and then dig and refine my search terms based on the type of event being sought.

From the perspective of a business, I would open the **Google keyword planner** and consult the "Get search volume and forecasts" section. Once there, you can jump to the "Keyword ideas" section and try different keywords.

- Write "Event planners" and click/tap "Get started";

- On the new page that will show up, you will input your search criteria;

- In this case you would select London, United Kingdom;

- Choose whether to get search results from Google only or from its search partners as well;

- Enter the search period.

The following image shows an extract taken from Google keyword planner

New form of payment required - Your current payment methods can't be charged

Keyword ideas
Forecast
Keyword plan
Saved keywords
Negative keywords

Q event planners

⊙ London, England, United Kingdom   文 English   ⊞ Google and search partners   🗓 Sept 2021 - Aug 2022

Broaden your search: + wedding planner + event organiser + event management company + catering company + corporate event planning + party planning

Exclude adult ideas ✕   Add filter   484 keyword ideas available

Keyword view ▾   Refine

Expand all

Brand or Non-Brands

Others

Keyword (by relevance)	Avg. monthly searches	Three month change	YoY change	Competition	Ad impression share	Top of page bid (low range)
event planners	1K – 10K	0%	+900%	Low	–	£0.83
Keyword ideas						
wedding planner	1K – 10K	0%	0%	High	–	£0.64
meeting planner	1K – 10K	0%	0%	Low	–	£0.84
wedding organizer	10 – 100	0%	0%	High	–	£0.56
event organizer	100 – 1K	0%	0%	Medium	–	£0.62
party planner	100 – 1K	0%	0%	Medium	–	£0.60
event coordinator	150 – 1K	0%	0%	Low	–	£0.21

Google Keyword Planner

For the year to Aug 2022, Google shows a monthly search of 1k to 10k, which means, on average in any month, users searched for event planners between 1 and 10 thousand times.

What's more, the YoY appears to be +900% and the competition is low, which means there was a huge increase (most probably due to the pandemic restrictions being eased) in searches compared to the previous year and not many event planning businesses are now advertising (on Google), this ultimately meaning there's potentially a nice market share which could be taken there!

If you then click on "Keyword ideas" and insert again your search criteria, Google will return your keywords as well as a number of similar alternatives, providing further ideas as to what people looked for over the previous year. In our case, it will return "wedding planners", which interestingly shows high competition amongst advertisers; "meeting planners", which has instead low competition; "party planner" with medium competition; "wedding event planner" which shows a 900% YoY and 3-month increase and medium competition; and many more keyword ideas for you to learn from.

Bear in mind competition here means competition on the specific keyword, not on the product per se, so the very same product might have high competition if you were advertising with certain keywords and low competition if you used different keywords.

For example, when I type solar panels with search area set to US, the exact keyword shows average monthly searches between 100k and 1m and high competition; "solar companies near me" between 10k and 100k searches and low competition. Nonetheless, many solar panel-related keywords are marked by high competition and a relatively high advert cost-per-click, this clearly meaning the competition is rather fierce.

Hopefully, the above example has given you some insight into the enlightening and powerful tool that Google Keyword Planner is. Certainly, we are not so naïve to think none of those searches came from other businesses trying to study their competitors but, most likely, the vast majority were carried out by potential customers and that is where the opportunities lie.

Facebook Ads

Even though Facebook is not as popular now as it used to be, it is still the most used social network and is together with Instagram, giving you access to an enormous potential prospect base. What's more, FB's powerful Ads customisation features can offer a great insight into your market.

Upon creating your ad, you'll have the opportunity to customise the audience, in other words your potential customer base.

Let's put we are launching a football/soccer pitch renting business in Wimbledon, Greater London.

Guys who, like me, love playing football with friends, are always on the lookout for new pitches to hire. So, where would I likely find out about new pitches, other than Google? Facebook could well be, because as I'm scrolling down on my mobile in the evening, I may be happy to come across adverts about football pitches in the area.

Moving on to the other end of the game, as a soon-to-launch business owner I would indeed check out FB Ads to both learn about my market and actually find customers.

The criteria available are age, location, gender, and detailed targeting which includes demographics, interest, and behaviour.

You could select men, aged between 18 and 45, with interest in football, who are based within a radius of 3km from an exact point which you can drop on the map.

FB's estimate audience size shows: 6.3K-7.4K. So, theoretically, you could reach between 6 and 7.4 thousand men aged 18 and 45 who have expressed interest in football over the previous 30 days.

Edit audience ✕

18 ──────●━━━━━━━━━━━━━━●────── 45

Selecting an audience under 18 will limit your targeting options to location, age and gender. Learn more

Locations ⓘ

🔍 Locations
Type to add more locations

United Kingdom

(51.4087, -0.2457) + 3 km ✕

Detailed targeting ⓘ
Your ad will be shown to people who match at least one of the following interests.

🔍 Detailed targeting
Search interests   Browse →

Interests

Football ✕

Audience definition
Your audience is defined.

Specific ━━━━━━━━━━━━━ Broad

Estimated audience size: 6.3K-7.4K ⓘ

Cancel   Save audience

FaceBook Ads editing window

Whilst not all of them will be playing football, a good part of that base could yet convert into paying customers.

FB business page will offer further refining features allowing you to narrow (or broaden) your target audience, but you have already got the sense of this. You will be able to save your audience and indeed edit it as you later improve your targeting.

Amazon

Started as a simple portal selling books, Amazon is now the major online sale platform in the world, a global brand recognised everywhere that built its success also thanks to a business model whereby everyone can get into business and sell their products on there. The advantage is double-sided as the business benefits from displaying its products on a most popular platform and Amazon gets a commission on each item sold on top of its monthly fees (charged regardless of the sales).

As Amazon kept growing, more small businesses saw the immense opportunity offered by this giant virtual shopping mall and, the more joined, the fiercer the competition. For users, this has meant wider product ranges, better quality, more options, and lower prices.

Despite the overall competition, there are still lots of opportunities on there so, if you are planning on selling physical or digital products online, Amazon should be taken into serious consideration. If not to sell on there, at least to do some market research. Yep, because analysing how a certain product sells on Amazon will help you establish if it has potential to sell elsewhere, too.

Let's suppose you want to sell kitchen towels made with recycled paper in the US – not a so easy sector, by the way, and you'll soon see why.

There is a very useful app called JungleScout, which can be installed as an add-on extension to Google Chrome and Firefox and generates nearly instant statistics on many, many items sold on Amazon, with information regarding monthly sales, daily sales, revenues, and net profits (net of Amazon's fees), all within a few seconds.

After you have installed the extension, go on amazon.com and type in "Recycled kitchen towel". As the relating list of products is populated open the JungleScout extension and wait for the records to be itemised.

The JS window will show you the statistics of the same items appearing on the Amazon page along with the sales data, which will give you an instant idea of whether your to-sell product is demanded for or not and how the competitors are doing. Not only, at the top-right corner is an index called "Opportunity score" which assigns a score to the listing based on how the demand and the competition are doing: 1 is lowest and 10 is the highest point given.

Returning on our example, JS assigns an opportunity score of 3 to recycled kitchen towel, which makes it a not so appealing product line to go for, at least on Amazon, since the competition is extremely high.

You may find items that are not exactly what you were looking for, in such cases you will have to refine your search until you have a neat enough list.

| | All ▾ | recycled kitchen towels | | | | | | | 🔍 | EN ▾ | Hello, Alessandro Account & Lists ▾ |

☰ Menu   JungleScout

Average Monthly Sales	Average Sales Rank	Average Price	Average Rating Number	Opportunity Score ⓘ
4,944	94,410	$24.71	4,680	③ High Demand with high comp.

	Actions ●	Product Name	Brand	Price	Mo. Sales	D. Sales	Mo. Revenue	Date First Available	Net
1	⊕ 🔖 ◊	EcoFirst Recycled Paper Towels ... B08FF6W588	EcoFirst	$6.99	4,588	179	$27,482	08/01/2020	$-0.92
2	⊕ 🔖 ◊	Seventh Generation Unbleached... B00C43H694	Seventh Ge...	$57.96	1,427	54	$82,709	03/30/2013	$20.19
×	⊕ 🔖 ◊	Seventh Generation Paper Towel... B004GSRHEM	Seventh Ge...	$63.60	1,650	36	$105,449	12/10/2010	$27.64
4	⊕ 🔖 ◊	Recycled Cotton Kitchen Towels... B09QSFWKS6	QUILTINA	$12.99	660	23	$8,573	04/02/2022	$7.27
5	⊕ 🔖 ◊	Candy Cottons Kitchen Towels S... B09WQKK429	Candy Cott...	$14.99	864	48	$12,951	03/28/2022	$7.6
6	⊕ 🔖 ◊	Reel Premium Recycled Paper T... B09N7F6ZQN	REEL	$47.99	1,797	56	$86,238	12/09/2021	$21.59
7	⊕ 🔖 ◊	365 by Whole Foods Market, Pa... B07QMW9YJV	365 by Wh...	$7.99	1	0	$8	09/23/2019	$-4.63
	⊕ 🔖 ◊	365 by Whole Foods Market, Pa...	365 by Wh...	$4.79	0	0	$0	09/23/2019	$-3.23

Showing Results 1 - 96   [Load More]

By clicking on a specific item, JS will also show you the monthly sales history of the product!

I find this feature of extreme help since viewing sales over a long enough period is one of the best indicators of how a product, whether it is from direct or indirect competition, is really wanted by people and how seasonal it is.

JungleScout: a product historic monthly sales

Virtually all items included in the parent categories are ranked by JungleScout, and by doing some research you will find ones with good opportunity scores where unmet customer needs can direct you towards profitable ideas.

If you then log in to your JS account (not the extension but on the JS website), you will have another wide range of features including Product research, Supplier, Marketing, Analytics and so on.

The opportunity finder within the Product research tab allows to search by many variables such as category, seasonality, competition, and even by keyword. One note here: the niche score is not the same as the opportunity score in the browser extension.

Marketing portals and trading associations

Portals such as Statista and Mintel offer statistics and reports on many business sectors divided by region or worldwide. Some of them are for free whilst others are for payment or are included in monthly or annual subscription plans. Complete with intuitive diagrams, reports can go into detail and give a clue as to who the major players in any given sector are.

Trading associations can also come your way providing you with reports on the sector you wish to start in.

Obtaining reports that provide sales volumes and revenues for your target market, ideally per each provider, will give you a real snapshot of the current market and help you craft your forecasts.

THE COMPETITION

Easy as it can be to get taken away with your business idea and, rightly so, for your enthusiasm to go sky-high – which is a very good thing – you must never forget to stay with your feet on the ground.

As much as our latest intuition has great potential, we should always analyse how the competition is doing. And, yes, even where the proposed idea is an innovative one, there will always be some degree of competition or some alternative products/services that already satisfy the perceived customer need.

Your competition can be direct or indirect, or both. Direct means there are competitors offering the same type of product/service you intend to sell; indirect is where you offer an innovative product or service and competitors already offer alternative solutions (but not the same product as you) for the customers' need. Whatever the need or wish of prospective customers, they always have options available to satisfy that need.

How many direct competitors are there? How many could there be in the future? Remember that the lower the barrier to entry in a market, the easier for other businesses to enter and make the competition fiercer.

What are they offering? What is their pricing? What is the total size of your market and what are the competitors' market shares?

In studying your market, you will need to assess the competitive intensity, intensity which is the result of not only the rivalry between businesses but also the threat of new entrants, how easy it is for customers to switch to alternative solutions, the bargaining power that customers have, the power of suppliers. All these factors can make the competition tougher or easier.

Depending on the type of product/service you intend to sell, you may want to refer to the previous chapter about JungleScout. A Google search will also help you find your competitors. And remember to pay attention to the customer ratings and reviews! Yep, because they will give you an overview of the other businesses' pluses and minuses, and help you understand where the offer can be improved, what customers like about a certain product, what their purchasing criteria are, and, last but certainly not least, how easy that market is to access – if customers are already happy with the current providers, why would they buy from a new one? Instead, chances are that a sector where there's demand but the current offer leaves customers unhappy will present plenty of opportunities to new businesses to enter (low entry barriers) and grow their market share. In this respect, review platforms such as Trustpilot lend a hand.

For your business plan to be reliable, you will have to include a chapter apart describing your competition, how intense it is, the competitors' pricing, their market share, their key success factors, their key financial data, their work force. In that ecosystem you will soon be part. And to persuade any investor, granting body or lending institution, you will have to show your path to success, so your plan.

And remember: Your new business will need to have some competitive advantage compared to the others, be it in terms of novelty of your product, lower selling price (while generating large enough margin and good profits at least in the long run), quality of your product, better marketing plan, better distribution, or a new promising market or region.

FORECASTING YOUR SALES

The eternal dilemma: how do you forecast your sales?

Let's start from acknowledging that nobody has the crystal ball, thus forecasting a business's sales entails doing what the word says: forecasting. In other words, making a realistic and justified estimate of the sales volumes and revenues for your business over the next three to five-years.

This involves considering your market size and your competitors, as a first point. It wouldn't make sense to predict sales for 10,000 pieces a month at the end of the first year if the market demand accounts for a total of 20,000 a month, that would mean you were assuming you would take half the market in the space of one year...

Your forecasts should also be justified as you will have to be able to explain to any querying investor how you got to this or that figure.

But before moving forward, there's a caveat: your sales estimate table should start from when your business is effectively operational. In other words, month 1 in your business plan should be when the business is ready to roll. If you expect to open your shop in six months, your month 1 will start then. There is no point in starting the clock when your business doesn't yet have the required licenses or essential machineries are not yet available.

This specified, how to work out your sales estimates then?

There are two main methods you can go for: top-down forecasting or bottom-up forecasting.

Top-down forecasting: from the overall sales volume in your target market, you estimate a little percentage for your business. To do this, put down the market shares of each competitor until you get to 100% - the minor players can be grouped into a single category.

From which competitor are you more likely to win customers from? Perhaps from a couple of them? If the market is expected to grow – you can find out by reading specialist forecasts which you can find in marketing portals, or online by googling them – you can assume a fraction of new customers will go to you.

For example, you are soon launching a product which is now sold by 8 competitors, the overall sales volume is 250,000 items per month. Some customers are unhappy with their current supplier/seller and would be keen to try a new one. To not overcomplicate the example, we will assume the market in question is relatively stable over the year so is not seasonal.

Let's put these are the market shares at the moment:

CURRENT MARKET				
Competitor	Market share	Monthly sales volume (items)	Average price	Sales revenue per month
Competitor 1	35%	87,500	£22.00	£1,925,000
Competitor 2	25%	62,500	£20.50	£1,281,250
Competitor 3	17%	42,500	£21.00	£892,500
Competitor 4	13%	32,500	£23.00	£747,500
Competitors 5, 6, 7, and 8	10%	25,000	£24.00	£600,000
Totals	100%	250,000	-	-

Market shares table

After a few initial months of relatively low sales, we could assume that at month 12 our business will have taken from the last competitors, say, 1% from their market therefore selling around 2,500 items a month, this meaning the market share of competitors 5 to 9 would shrink to 9%.

Assuming our business makes customers happy so more of them will come thanks to word of mouth and good reviews, we might forecast a steady sales growth on each month.

If we then suppose recent experts' predictions forecast an overall growth of our market by, say, 10% per year, we might add a further 10% to our 1% share.

Of course, the above is just a simplified example of how the top-down method would work. In reality, you would need to evaluate your main competitors' strengths and weaknesses, check if they have reviews to understand what extent of unhappy customers they have, understand why they are so good at what they do, what their annual accounts say, how they market their business, and so on.

In addition, for a more accurate business plan, you would carry out the above exercise for each product / market segment. So, if you intended to sell shoes and similar to customers of different ages, you would prepare for example one forecast for sports shoes for customers aged 5-10; one for sports shoes for customers aged 11 over; one for school shoes; one for elegant shoes young adults not for school; one for elegant shoes for office customers; etc; and finally you would add all segments together to have the full picture.

As you can imagine, much would depend on the availability of sectorial market reports. The more in-depth the report(s) is/are, the more accurate your forecast (and your budgeting) will be.

Bottom-up forecasting: this type of forecasting requires a little more ingenious work as you will have to build an estimate on the different sales funnels available to you (again, ideally for each product/market segment) and add all estimate figures together, whereas a sales funnel is any of the channels through which your potential customers get to know about your business, evaluate your products and decide whether to buy or not. In this sense, FB Ads is a sales funnel, Amazon is another, so are sales portals, Google search results...

A word of caution here, certain funnels work better in some industries and less well in others. For example, if you were starting an online food delivery kitchen, Amazon would certainly not be your sales funnel, as opposed to platforms such as Deliveroo, JustEat and UberEats as well as FB.

Hypothesizing your food delivery business is going to be located in Hackney, London, UK, you would create a working spreadsheet such as this one which I prepared for a client of mine.

The product / market segments expected to bring revenue were identified as the following:

> Ready meals for families and individuals;

> Ready meals for offices;

> Cook-at-home boxes for families and individuals;

> Cooking master classes online;

> Cooking master classes offline.

To each of the above I assigned the appropriate sales funnels and summed up the resulting figures to obtain the estimate monthly sales. Since the type of business in question is not seasonal, we expected the figures to remain stable over the months and a prudential growth coefficient would be applied (as the business would get known among new customers).

Please see the following extract:

READY MEALS - INDIVIDUALS / FAMILIES

	Women aged 24+ with interest in Italian cuisine, Italian resturant, pasta - 2miles of Karma Hackney - eligible to see your ad based on previous 30 days			
Facebook Ads	Potential audience	31,000		
	Average click-through rate (CTR) for FB Ads by industry: retail	1.59%		
	Est avg clicks	493	Avg FB cost per click (CPC) in retail	£0.56
	Est conversion rate FB Ads in retail	2.28%		
	Est avg monthly conversions (orders)	**11**	**Est total FB monthly cost**	**£276.02**
Deliveroo	Web traffic deliveroo.co.uk April 2020	7,300,000		
	Bounce rate	34.02%		
	Net traffic rate	65.98%		
	Net traffic	4,816,540		
	Est proportion to 3km area around Karma Hackney (1/238)	20,238		
	Est CTR	3.80%		
	Est clicks	769		
	Est conversion rate	2.10%		
	Est avg monthly conversions (orders)	**16**		
JustEat	Web traffic justeat.co.uk April 2020	25,200,000		
	Bounce rate	34.72%		
	Net traffic rate	65.28%		
	Net traffic	16,450,560		
	Est proportion to 3km area around Karma Hackney (1/238)	69,120		
	Est CTR	3.80%		
	Est clicks	2,627		
	Est conversion rate	2.10%		
	Est avg monthly conversions (orders)	**55**		

TOTALS READY MEALS INDIVIDUALS / FAMILIES: EST MONTHLY CONVERSI   83

READY MEALS - OFFICES

	People aged 25 to 64 with interest in Italian cuisine, pasta or Italian restaurant - within 3km of Karma Hackney - eligible to see ad based on previous 30 days				
Facebook Ads	Potential audience	41,000			
	% employed in London March 2020	68.29%			
	Est people in employment in relevant area	27,998			
	Est people in work days in rel area	19,998			
	Average CTR for FB Ads by industry: retail	1.59%			
	Est avg clicks	318	Avg FB cost per click (CPC) in retail	£0.56
	Est conversion rate FB Ads in retail	2.28%			
	Est avg monthly conversions (orders)	**7**	**Total est monthly FB cost**	**£178.07**
Deliveroo	**Web traffic deliveroo.co.uk April 2020**	7,300,000			
	Bounce rate	34.02%			
	Net traffic rate	65.98%			
	Net traffic	4,816,540			
	Est proportion to 3km area around Karma Hackney (1/238)	20,238			
	% employed in London March 2020	68.29%			
	Est people in employment in relevant area	13,820			
	Est visits in work days	9,871			
	Est CTR	3.80%			
	Est clicks	375			
	Est conversion rate	2.10%			
	Est avg monthly conversions (orders)	**8**			
JustEat	**Web traffic justeat.co.uk April 2020**	25,200,000			
	Bounce rate	34.72%			
	Net traffic rate	65.28%			
	Net traffic	16,450,560			
	Est proportion to 3km area around Karma Hackney (1/238)	69,120			
	% employed in London March 2020	68.29%			
	Est people in employment in relevant area	47,200			
	Est visits in work days	33,714			
	Est CTR	3.80%			
	Est clicks	1,281			
	Est conversion rate	2.10%			
	Est avg monthly conversions (orders)	**27**			
READY MEALS - OFFICES	**Est avg monthly conversions / orders**	**42**			

COOK-AT-HOME

Facebook Ads	Women aged 24+ with interest in Italian cuisine, pasta or pasta recipes - England - eligible to see ad based on previous 30 days			
	Potential audience	2,400,000		
	Average CTR for FB Ads by industry: retail	1.59%		
	Avg potential clicks	38,160	Avg FB cost per click (CPC) in retail	£0.56
	Est monthly click cap	32,143	Monthly spend cap	£18,000.00
	Est conversion rate FB Ads in retail	2.28%		
	Est avg monthly conversions (orders)	734	Total est monthly FB cost	£18,000.00

TOTALS COOK-AT-HOME	Est monthly conversions (orders)	734

MASTER CLASSES OFFLINE

FB Ads	People 18+ with interest in cooking, cooking classes, baking and recipes - London - eligible to see ad based on previou			
	Potential audience	2,600,000		
	Average CTR for FB Ads by industry: education	0.73%		
	Est avg potential clicks	18,980	Avg FB cost per click (CPC) in education	£0.85
	Est monthly click cap	2,941	Monthly spend cap	£2,500.00
	Est conversion rate FB Ads in education	2.72%		
	Est avg monthly conversions (orders)	80	Total est monthly FB cost	£2,500.00

MASTER CLASSES OFFLINE	Estimate total monthly conversions	80

MASTER CLASSES ONLINE

FB Ads	People 18+ with interest in cooking, cooking classes, baking and recipes - United Kingdom - eligible to see ad based on			
	Potential audience	20,000,000		
	Average CTR for FB Ads by industry: education	0.73%		
	Est avg potential clicks	146,000	Avg FB cost per click (CPC) in education	£0.85
	Est monthly click cap	2,941	Monthly spend cap	£2,500.00
	Est conversion rate FB Ads in education	2.72%		
	Est avg monthly conversions (orders)	80	Total est monthly FB cost	£2,500.00

MASTER CLASSES ONLINE	Estimate total monthly conversions	80

As shown above, these workings will not only render realistic estimates of your sales but also help you work out the variable portion of your advertising costs (which will end up in your budgeting).

For space reasons, I could not include the whole screenshot, but in the plan were also the sources of any statistics I put in. Including the sources of your data is important as it will substantiate the idea that the forecasts were made with method.

Once you have built your expected initial figures, you can work out your monthly and yearly sales projections, whereas these are typically made up of a first-year month-by-month sales estimate and a three-year year-by-year estimate.

Following are the first-year sales projections for the food delivery business. Again for space reasons, I only include the first months but you will nonetheless have to complete the exercise for the whole year.

Sales estimate 1st year	Price per portion	Month 1			Month 2			Month 3		
DISHES		Month var %	Portion s sold	Sales	Month unit var %	Portion s sold	Sales	Month unit var %	Portion s sold	Sales
Ready-to-Eat for Families/Individuals										
Focaccia	£3.00	-	119	£357	6%	126	£378	6%	134	£401
Melanzane alla parmigiana	£9.00	-	99	£892	6%	105	£945	6%	111	£1,002
Pappardelle al ragù	£8.70	-	79	£690	6%	84	£731	6%	89	£775
Troccoli con sugo di calamari	£13.00	-	20	£258	6%	21	£273	6%	22	£289
Gnocchi di patate, burro e salvia	£6.00	-	20	£119	6%	21	£126	6%	22	£134
Chocolate and ricotta tart	£4.85	-	59	£288	6%	63	£306	6%	67	£324
TOTAL Ready-to-Eat for Families/Individuals		-	396	£2,602		420	£2,759		445	£2,924
Ready-to-Eat for Offices										
Focaccia	£3.00	-	25	£76	6%	27	£80	6%	28	£85
Melanzane alla parmigiana	£9.00	-	21	£189	6%	22	£201	6%	24	£213
Pappardelle al ragù	£8.70	-	17	£146	6%	18	£155	6%	19	£164
Troccoli con sugo di calamari	£13.00	-	4	£55	6%	4	£58	6%	5	£61
Gnocchi di patate, burro e salvia	£6.00	-	4	£25	6%	4	£27	6%	5	£28
Chocolate and ricotta tart	£4.85	-	13	£61	6%	13	£65	6%	14	£69
TOTAL Ready-to-Eat for Offices		-	84	£552		89	£585		94	£620
Cook-at-Home Pasta										
Pappardelle al ragù	£7.81	-	1,056	£8,249	6%	1,120	£8,744	6%	1,187	£9,269
Troccoli con sugo di calamari	£11.00	-	528	£5,809	6%	560	£6,158	6%	593	£6,527
Gnocchi di patate, burro e salvia	£6.00	-	704	£4,225	6%	746	£4,478	6%	791	£4,747
Orecchiette al sugo pomodoro fresco con r	£6.25	-	528	£3,301	6%	560	£3,499	6%	593	£3,709
Troccoli alla norma	£7.87	-	352	£2,771	6%	373	£2,937	6%	396	£3,113
Ravioli alla genovese	£12.00	-	352	£4,225	6%	373	£4,478	6%	396	£4,747
TOTAL Cook-at-Home Pasta		-	3,521	£28,580		3,732	£30,295		3,956	£32,113

Sales forecast first months 1/3

Sales estimate 1st year CLASSES OFFLINE	Avg revenue	Month 1			Month 2			Month 3		
		Month var %	Units sold	Sales	Month unit var %	Units sold	Sales	Month unit var %	Units sold	Sales
Classes Offline Pasta										
Pasta fresca cookery	£650.00	-	3	£2,253	0%	3	£2,253	0%	3	£2,253
Pasta fresca cookery Pro	£890.00	-	3	£3,085	0%	3	£3,085	0%	3	£3,085
Total Classes Offline Pasta			7	£5,339		7	£5,339		7	£5,339
Classes Offline Pasta at Home										
Pasta Master class at home - pasta only	£600.00	-	3	£1,560	0%	3	£1,560	0%	3	£1,560
Pasta Master class at home - complete me	£780.00	-	3	£2,028	0%	3	£2,028	0%	3	£2,028
Total Classes Offline Pasta at Home			5	£3,588		5	£3,588		5	£3,588
Classes Offline Corporates	£1,500.00	-	2	£2,600	0%	2	£2,600	0%	2	£2,600
Classes Offline Kids	£300.00		3	£1,040	0%	3	£1,040	0%	3	£1,040
TOTAL Classes Offline Pasta			17	£12,567		17	£12,567		17	£12,567

Sales forecast first months 2/3

40

Sales estimate 1st year CLASSES ONLINE	Avg revenue	Month 1			Month 2			Month 3		
		Month var %	Units sold	Sales	Month unit var %	Units sold	Sales	Month unit var %	Units sold	Sales
Classes Online (Single Courses)										
Pasta fresca cookery	£18.00	-	24	£431	2%	24	£440	2%	25	£449
Pasta dish by Italian region	£18.00	-	24	£431	2%	24	£440	2%	25	£449
Pasticceria italiana basic	£18.00	-	8	£144	2%	8	£147	2%	8	£150
Pasticceria italiana advanced	£18.00	-	12	£216	2%	12	£220	2%	12	£224
Lievito madre and house planning	£18.00	-	8	£144	2%	8	£147	2%	8	£150
Total Classes Online (Single Courses)		-	76	£1,366		77	£1,393		79	£1,421
Classes Online (All-Course Package)	£150.00	-	4	£599	2%	4	£611	2%	4	£623
Total Classes Online (Single Courses)			80	£1,965		81	£2,004		83	£2,044
Overall total sales 1st year				£46,266.50			£48,209.89			£50,268.31

Sales forecast first months 3/3

Three-year sales projections

Product/service lines	1st year				2nd year				3rd year			
	Portions/classes sold *	Orders	Yrly change %	Revenue	Portions/classes sold *	Orders	Yrly change %	Revenue	Portions/classes sold *	Orders	Yrly change %	Revenue
Dishes												
Ready-to-Eat for Families/Individuals	6,685	1,393	-	£43,904	8,156	1,699	22.00%	£53,562	8,808	1,835	8.00%	£57,847
Ready-to-Eat for Offices	1,418	295	-	£9,315	1,730	360	22.00%	£11,364	1,869	389	8.00%	£12,273
Cook-at-Home Pasta	59,396	12,374	-	£482,145	72,463	15,096	22.00%	£588,216	78,260	16,304	8.00%	£635,274
Total Dishes	**67,499**	**14,062**		**£535,363**	**82,349**	**17,156**	**22.00%**	**£653,143**	**88,937**	**18,528**	**8.00%**	**£705,394**
Classes												
Classes Offline												
Classes Offline Pasta	83	-		£64,064	87	-	4.00%	£66,627	89	-	2.50%	£68,292
Classes Offline Pasta at Home	62	-		£43,056	65	-	4.00%	£44,778	67	-	2.50%	£45,898
Classes Offline Corporates	21	-		£31,200	22	-	4.00%	£32,448	22	-	2.50%	£33,259
Classes Offline Kids	42	-		£12,480	43	-	4.00%	£12,979	44	-	2.50%	£13,304
Total Classes Offline	**208**			**£150,800**	**216**		**4.00%**	**£156,832**	**222**		**2.50%**	**£160,753**
Classes Online												
Classes Online (Single Courses)	1,018	-		£18,321	1,059	-	4.00%	£19,054	1,085	-	2.50%	£19,530
Classes Online (All-Course Package)	54	-		£8,035	56	-	4.00%	£8,357	57	-	2.50%	£8,566
Total Classes Online	**1,071**			**£26,356**	**1,114**		**4.00%**	**£27,410**	**1,142**		**2.50%**	**£28,096**
Total Classes	**1,279**			**£177,156**	**1,331**			**£184,242**	**1,364**			**£188,848**
Total Overall	**-**			**£712,519**			**17.52%**	**£837,385**			**6.79%**	**£894,243**

WHAT YOUR BUSINESS PLAN SHOULD INCLUDE

A business plan is a comprehensive document setting out the path of a new or growing business into the future.

It is typically drafted in the view of pitching to investors and raise funds, but it also represents an extremely useful tool for managers and owners for setting their business's goals and objectives and monitoring performance over time.

Sometimes confused with pitch deck, a business plan will include a set of descriptive sections and the financial projections over the next three to five years.

The descriptive sections comprise the following elements as a minimum: executive summary, goals and objectives, market demand, competition analysis, sales forecast, marketing strategy.

There is no right or wrong answer as to how long the sections should be other than they should not be too longwinded nor too concise. The wording should be simple, but technical where necessary, so to make the reading catching and the reader confident about your expertise.

Whether you are facing an investor, a lender, or a granting body, it is paramount that you show them upon which data, statistics, analyses, or trends you have based your forecasts, and provide them with a breakdown wherever applicable.

The financial projections generally comprise cash flow, sales forecast, income statements, profit & loss, stock, financial ratios, assets, and any other relevant forecast elements.

Since a business plan is essentially based on predictions closely related to the financial projections, you want to make sure these are formulated with care and skill.

Strategic, proactive, realistic. These are the three words I would say to anyone looking to embark on a new business venture.

Do your part, analyse your whole idea and then, once you are happy with the result, put it down in words (and figures) into a great business plan!

Here are the main sections you should have in your plan:

1. Executive Summary

The executive summary introduces the reader to the founders and their start-up. Normally beginning with a general presentation, the reader here will have a chance to learn about the business idea, what the goals and objectives are, how the entrepreneurs intend to achieve them.

This will be followed by a section about the personal background of the founders, including their education and their business / work experience with particular emphasis on what is related to the start-up in question and what makes its creators investable resources.

A start-up summary should then provide an overview of your starting enterprise and its business model, business model which should brief the reader about the way your business will operate and be profitable. You should answer the first basic question: how will it make money? For details about its profitability, you will direct to the financial projections

2. Products / services offered

This section will lay out the product/service lines of your future business explaining what their characteristics are, who your target customers are, and detailing all your product/market segments and the pricing.

Say to your readers a reason why your offering is going to fill a gap in the current market, what will make your products a good choice and how you are qualified to create high-quality ones. If products are going to be sourced from other suppliers, explain this and what research you have done to identify the best suppliers.

While care should clearly be taken here to not give away too much information, especially in case of patent-protected ideas, some insight should be given into the processes to produce or source the selling products.

3.   Goals and Objectives

Here you should set out what you intend to achieve in the short and the long term, whereas goals typically refer to concepts and objectives to figures. So, for example, a goal could be to become a leader in your sector in five years while an objective might be to increase sales by 200% in two years. A goal may be to become a recognised brand among young customers, an objective could be about achieving a 40% market share within a certain period.

4. Market Analysis

4.1. Target customers

How are your target customers? Spell out their macro-characteristics such as their region, age, background, their purchasing criteria. Not only, divide your prospect base into business segments, i.e. product/market segments, taking into account that a product line may be directed to different markets. In your business plan, each business segment will represent a distinct income-generating unit having its own costing elements. For example, a team of chefs planning to start a home delivery restaurant also offering cook-at-home recipe boxes and cooking classes online and offline, will realise the ready-to-eat dishes area involve different pricing criteria and different costs than the cook-at-home boxes area, let alone the classes. Accordingly, they might determine the following business segments:

A) Ready-to-eat for home targeting people aged, say, 25 or over, who live nearby your restaurant;

B) Ready-to-eat for offices targeting firms based in your area;

C) Cook-at-home boxes for families, presumably targeting customers in an age group, say, 30 or over who are parents, how live within a certain radius from your restaurant (taking into account that food yet to cook can be served presumably anywhere reachable by van or car);

D) Pre-recorded online classes targeting families based anywhere;

E) Offline classes, targeting people living at reasonable distance from you.

4.2. Market Demand

Here you would bring in relevant statistics on what the demand was in the past and forecasts about future trends. Needless to say, those statistics and forecasts should come from authoritative bodies/firms, and make sure you cite the sources. If you were planning to start selling solar panels, the current energy crisis should be factored in as a powerful driver of future demand; accordingly, you might want to include graphs showing how the demand has gone up recently.

5. Competition

Referring to the section about the competition, you would list your competitors in each of your main business segments. So, returning on the example of the food delivery restaurant, different competitors will be out there when considering the ready-to-eat segments or the online classes.

6. Management and Personnel

If the founders are not going to be involved in the day-to-day business, add information about the initial manager(s) you have identified, what their background is and what makes them a good fit in your to-be firm.

If you expect to employ personnel, give details of how many you will bring in and what their responsibilities will be.

7. Marketing Strategy

What will your marketing strategy involve? Which sales funnels will you be using or, in other words, from which channels will your customers find you and buy?

Marketing includes getting your new brand known, communicating with prospective customers, sending out promotional material, and, last but not least, dealing with customers up to the sale stage. And beyond: Remember that post-sales assistance can prove crucial to establish and strengthen your brand's credibility.

As for your sales channels, depending on the sector and type of products (or services) offered, you will use FaceBook groups, Facebook Ads, or Google Ads, or Instagram, TikTok, or more traditional means such as flyers, leaflets, or other ways, or even better a combination of some of those.

All of the above should be put down in your business plan. And if you expect to take on personnel specifically for your marketing, I encourage you to add it to your plan.

In setting out your strategy, you will also specify how much you expect to spend on each of your funnels.

8.   Financial projections

Even though you will have a separate spreadsheet file with all your computations, you should include extracts of those computations in your business plan as well: this is where the investor will first look; if they then want to dig into the numbers, they will consult the spreadsheet for the full calculations.

This is what I suggest you include in your business plan:

- ➢ Expenses and Investments

- ➢ First-year monthly sales projections

- ➢ 3-year yearly sales projections

- ➢ First-year Cash flow projections

- ➢ Profit and loss for three years

- ➢ Financial ratios and main margins

Make sure you include relevant graphs and diagrams as these will give an immediate visual of your estimates.

The other computations such as balance sheet statements, amortisations and depreciations, funnel costings and so on would ideally go in a separate spreadsheet which you will keep available for inspection.

EXPENSES AND INVESTMENTS

First of all, what is the difference?

Expenses are incurred for items used within a short time or, in any case, within a year-time; investments, on the other hand, are made on assets that will produce long-term (over a year-time) benefit to the business.

Rental fees, legal and professional fees, bank charges, raw materials to manufacture your goods, are all expenses since the purchased items are typically used up continuously and, in any case, within a certain time, regardless of whether or not more will be purchased in the future.

Costs incurred for computers, property purchases, machinery or asset acquisitions are all investments as they will most likely be kept by your business for several years.

When estimating costs, you should take your time to write down all expenses and investments required to get your business up and running. Most likely, more will pop up in your mind at a later stage, write them down as they come along. What you want to achieve is a complete picture of all costs required.

On the next page is an extract taken from a business plan I prepared some time ago for a kids play centre.

Expenses	Year one	Year two	Year three
Legal/administrative			
Accountancy & payroll	£1,200.00	£1,200.00	£1,200.00
Interest on business loan	£3,291.15	£2,604.25	£1,896.44
Registration with ICO (for data protection)	£40.00	£40.00	£40.00
Tills software and maintenance	£864.00	£864.00	£864.00
Compliance (annual)			
Training courses for personnel	£300.00	£300.00	£300.00
Premises and licences			
Premises rental	£24,000.00	£24,000.00	£24,000.00
Public liability insurance	£2,000.00	£2,000.00	£2,000.00
Business rates	£6,975.00	£6,975.00	£6,975.00
Electricity bills	£5,400.00	£5,400.00	£5,400.00
Gas bills	£2,160.00	£2,160.00	£2,160.00
Water bills	£1,440.00	£1,440.00	£1,440.00
Advertising			
Banners	£240.00	£240.00	£240.00
Facebook ads	£960.00	£960.00	£960.00
Website	£288.00	£288.00	£288.00
Other expenses			
Food and beverages for parties	£800.00	£800.00	£800.00
Building and content insurance	£360.00	£360.00	£360.00
Stationery	£120.00	£120.00	£120.00
Cleaning products	£1,000.00	£1,000.00	£1,000.00
Personnel			
Full-time staff: 1	£19,433.40	£19,433.40	£19,433.40
Part-time staff: 1	£9,716.70	£9,716.70	£9,716.70
Head chef: 1 part-time	£11,243.44	£11,243.44	£11,243.44
Contingent liabilities			
Reparings	£1,500.00	£1,500.00	£1,500.00
Total expenses	**£93,331.69**	**£92,644.79**	**£91,936.98**

Expenses estimate for kids play centre

As opposed to the above-mentioned expenses, further ahead are illustrated the estimated start-up investments.

Start-up investments	Amounts
Legal/administrative	
Company formation	£15.00
Business advice	£300.00
Tills	£1,200.00
Compliance	
Health & safety fire exits	£600.00
Health & safety equipment	£450.00
DBS checks on personnel	£210.00
Equipment	
Inflatables	£10,200.00
Toddler play equipment	£3,000.00
Baby equipment	£2,400.00
Tables & chairs	£1,080.00
Carpet tiles	£720.00
Kitchen fit-out	£30,000.00
Other investments	
CCTV	£420.00
Signage	£480.00
Miscellaneous	
Uniforms for personnel	£180.00
Total start-up investments	**£51,255.00**

Start-up Investments for kids play centre

Again, investments are expected to be made on a one-off basis as will be repeated after several years. You may want to move some minor ones (such as company formation in this example) to expenses because of the irrelevant figure. Indeed, some professionals prefer doing so if it is about petty amounts.

One important aspect to keep in mind is that amounts for expenses and investments are typically exclusive of VAT (since VAT payable is typically not a cost). However, if you do not expect to go over the annual turnover registration threshold (now at £85,000 turnover per year) and decide to not register your business for VAT, the amounts in your business plan will have to include VAT as the tax will indeed represent a cost just as much as the VATable net.

PROFITS AND LOSS PROJECTIONS

These are annual projections and include all expenses and the annual depreciation of your assets.

You would normally arrange the statements according to the following order:

Sales
- Refunds to customers
Net revenue
- Cost of goods sold
Gross profit/loss
- Other operating expenses
Operating profit/loss
- Assets amortisation/depreciation
- Interest payable
Profit/loss before tax
- Taxes
Net profit / loss

Profit and loss forecast headings

Sales correspond to revenue and do not include VAT.

Like it or not, there will be refunds to customers who are unhappy or change their mind after they are billed. It is reasonable to assume this will be more the case where you sell products rather than services, and this assumption is made on the empiric basis that products are often paid for in advance and a small percentage may present technical faults or customers can change their mind and return them. Services, on the other hand, are usually charged for in arrear and the conditions giving rise to a refund are far less likely to be met.

For products, you may want to assume around 2% of sales will be refunded, while for services you may assume a percentage ranging from 0.5% to 1%. Those percentages can clearly vary depending on the specific industry and type of products/services, so further judgement will be required.

The net revenue will be the algebraic sum of sales and refunds.

The cost of the goods sold, sometimes shortened to COGS, is the costs that are directly related to the products/services a business sells. They are the direct costs your business undergoes to manufacture/produce the products/services they sell over a certain year or period. For example, if you have a retail clothing shop, the COGS will be given by the total you have spent on all the pieces of clothing you sell during the period/year; it will also include the associated shipping costs, the packaging – if this is not already included in the item purchase cost – any direct labour costs, if applicable, and any portion of costs directly related to the goods / services sold.

Separate mention should be made of credit card and similar transaction fees: these are not strictly cost of goods sold but they will be put down right after the COGS to determine the total cost of sales.

Bear in mind the same principle applies whether you are working out your gross profit or your gross margin.

What is the difference, by the way? Gross profit relates to the entirety of the goods sold whilst the margin refers to the single item, so the gross profit equates to the sum of the gross margins of all items sold.

The gross profit formula is:

Sales – COGS – Transaction fees = Gross Profit

The gross margin formula:

Item sales price − Item direct costs − Transaction fee = Gross margin

The operating expenses, OPEX in short, are expenses incurred during the normal business operations but not directly related to the sold products/services. OPEXs cannot be allocated against a certain product or category of products sold by your business.

Think, for example, of the difference between ingredients' expenses and rental fees in an Italian restaurant.

The cost of ingredients falls within the COGS as it is directly correlated with the dishes you sell: to prepare pizza you buy the flour just as to prepare tiramisu you buy the mascarpone, and those expenses can certainly be allocated against your sold products.

On the other hand, regardless of what dishes you prepare for your customers and, indeed, regardless of the quantity sold, rental fees will still be applicable as it was not the lasagne nor the pizzas nor the tiramisus in particular that required you to use (and pay) your venue; you might even switch to Indian cuisine and the rental will still be the same.

Similar to rental fees, employee wages, utility bills, accounting fees, legal fees, business rates, insurances, advertising and marketing, are all operating expenses.

If you subtract the operating expenses from the gross profit, you will obtain the operating profit:

Gross Profit – OPEX = Operating Profit

Now, returning on the investments (remember investments are made on assets, whether physical or intangible, which have a useful life of over a year), you will have to work out the portion of those investments to be allocated to each year.

Let's suppose you purchase a new industrial machine for £25,000 which will presumably have a useful life of five years - for simplifying, we will ignore VAT here and assume we made that purchase at the beginning of the financial year.

From an accounting point of view, on your balance sheet will be recorded a monetary outflow of £25,000 on one side and an increase in assets for, again, £25,000 on the other. However, at the end of the year, that machine will have lost value as a result of its normal obsolescence, and this will have to be accounted for. As we assumed the machine's useful life was five years, we will have to reduce the value of that asset by one fifth. In other words, at the end of the year it will have lost 20% of its economic value and will be worth £20,000. Said reduction, known as depreciation, will be recorded on the balance sheet as a direct reduction off the initial assets value and on the profit & loss as a depreciation cost for £5,000.

Depreciation, which is applied to physical assets, will have to be included in the P&L projections of your business plan, and so will the amortisation – which, instead, applies to non-physical or intangible assets such as licenses, software, goodwill etc.

Moving ahead with your business plan, you will list any foreseeable interest and other financial expenses.

Operating Profit – Depreciations & amortisations – Financial charges = Profit before tax

Once you have worked out all relevant amortisation and depreciation costs and included any interest charges, you will be able to calculate the profit/loss before tax, from which you will then subtract the corporation tax to determine the net profit/loss of the year.

Profit before tax – Corporation tax = Net profit/loss of the year

P&L projections, like the rest of the financial projections, would better cover a period from 3 to 5 years as per normal practice.

BALANCE SHEET

The Balance sheet will include year-by-year projections of the assets and liabilities as well as the equity section of your to-be business.

The assets will include non-current assets, i.e. assets which are kept by the business for years, and current assets, which typically include bank account balances and amounts due by debtors within the year. Although unlikely, in your business plan you might also have pre-payments and accruals.

The liabilities, instead, are debts and obligations that your business will owe to other parties, whether they are trade creditors, tax office, bond subscribers, etc...

Similarly to assets, liabilities are also divided into current liabilities which are due within the year and non-current ones, which are due after a year-time.

The equity is the total amount subscribed by the business owners, usually in the form of share capital if it is a company, added to any additional fundings and reserves and any retained earnings or deducted of any brought-forward losses.

The difference between assets and liabilities will have to correspond to the total equity amount. If this is not the case, there is an error somewhere in the computations and you will have to rectify it.

The following image shows an example of balance sheet for a home delivery restaurant business.

Year 0 corresponds to the moment when the business, after having collected the initial funding and made the first investments, is ready to start its operations.

Year 1, year 2 and year 3 mean respectively the end of the first, the second and the third operating year.

Balance sheet	Year 0	Year one	Year two	Year three
Non-current assets	**Year 0**	**Year one**	**Year two**	**Year three**
Legal/administrative	£2,295	£1,836	£1,377	£918
Shared equipment	£21,900	£17,520	£13,140	£8,760
Shared works	£10,000	£8,000	£6,000	£4,000
Virtual brands	£16,000	£12,800	£9,600	£6,400
Websites set-up	£8,000	£6,400	£4,800	£3,200
Deliveroo subscriptions	£3,200	£2,560	£1,920	£1,280
JustEat subscriptions	£3,200	£2,560	£1,920	£1,280
UberEats	£3,200	£2,560	£1,920	£1,280
Tandoori ovens	£1,600	£1,280	£960	£640
Gas cooker	£1,800	£1,440	£1,080	£720
8-burner cooker	£1,200	£960	£720	£480
Food prep & packag tables	£1,200	£960	£720	£480
Onion peeler	£500	£400	£300	£200
Kitchen canopies	£22,000	£17,600	£13,200	£8,800
Metal sinks	£2,000	£1,600	£1,200	£800
Advertising - initial campaigns FB	£14,000	£11,200	£8,400	£5,600
Advertising - initial campaigns Google Ads	£6,000	£4,800	£3,600	£2,400
Total non-current assets	**£118,095**	**£94,476**	**£70,857**	**£47,238**
Current assets	**Year 0**	**Year one**	**Year two**	**Year three**
Cash at bank and in hand	£3,286	£516,909	£1,316,192	£2,280,287
Debtors (due within year)	£23,619	£0	£0	£0
Total current assets	**£26,905**	**£516,909**	**£1,316,192**	**£2,280,287**
Total assets	**£145,000**	**£611,385**	**£1,387,049**	**£2,327,525**

Balance sheet assets forecast for three years

Further down is an extract of the same balance sheet listing the company's liabilities and equity.

The control results being zero mean the computations are correct.

Creditors (within the year)	Year 0	Year one	Year two	Year three
Trade creditors	£0	£1,000	£1,000	£1,000
Other creditors	£0	£124,396	£216,503	£275,227
Total current liabilities	£0	£125,396	£217,503	£276,227
Net current assets	£145,000	£485,989	£1,169,547	£2,051,298
Equity	Year 0	Year one	Year two	Year three
Share capital	£20,000	£20,000	£20,000	£20,000
Shareholders' additional fundings	£125,000	£125,000	£125,000	£125,000
Profit / loss	£0	£340,989	£683,557	£881,751
Retained earnings / loss brought forward	£0	£0	£340,989	£1,024,547
Total equity	£145,000	£485,989	£1,169,547	£2,051,298
Liabilities over the year	Year 0	Year one	Year two	Year three
Trade creditors	£0	£0	£0	£0
Other creditors over the year	£0	£0	£0	£0
Total liabilities over the year	£0	£0	£0	£0
Control		£0	£0	£0	£0

Balance sheet liabilities and equity forecast

CASH FLOW PROJECTIONS

Cash flows projections follow closely the expenses and investments and the forecast sales.

More precisely, expenses and investments regard the costs that your business undergoes to purchase merchandise, goods, assets and so on; the cash flows, instead, are the payments actually made for those purchases and will include VAT, if applicable.

For example, if I forecast buying merchandise at the price of £10 per unit (+ 20% VAT), the cost will be £10 whilst the relating cash outflow will be £12 as I will also pay the 20% VAT on top. As before, if my business is not expected to register for VAT, the cost to my business will be £12 per unit, so cash outflow and expense will be equal in this case.

Consideration apart should be made over investments as they are usually made once, on assets that last years. In this case, the cost will be spread over the expected duration of the asset so if, for example, I buy a computer for £1,000 + 20% VAT which is expected to last four years, I will have to operate a depreciation to it of 25% for each year of its duration. As a result, I will have an initial cash outflow of £1,200 and an annual depreciation (cost) of £250 per annum (£1,000 net investment divided by four years of expected duration).

Again, if my business is not going to be VAT-registered, the depreciation will be applied to the total £1,200 so that the cost will be £300 per year.

Same logic will follow sales projections and cash inflows projections, whereas sales will include your income without any applicable VAT and cash inflows will include the VAT which you cash in when selling your products.

As per the sales projections, cash flows should cover the first year on a month-by-month basis and then, usually, 3 to 5 years projections on a year-by-year basis.

Following is an extract of cash flow projections for the first three months.

Beginning balance		£0	£83,612	£77,306	£75,689
Cash inflows	**Month 0**	**Month 1**	**Month 2**	**Month 3**	
Ready-to-Eat for Families/Individuals		£3,123	£3,310	£3,509	
Ready-to-Eat for Offices		£663	£702	£744	
Cook-at-Home Pasta		£28,580	£30,295	£32,113	
Classes Offline Pasta		£6,406	£6,406	£6,406	
Classes Offline Pasta at Home		£4,306	£4,306	£4,306	
Classes Offline Corporates		£3,120	£3,120	£3,120	
Classes Offline Kids		£1,248	£1,248	£1,248	
Classes Online (Single Courses)		£1,639	£1,672	£1,705	
Classes Online (All-Course Package)		£719	£733	£748	
Owners' funding	£5,000	£0	£0	£0	
External funding	£80,000	£0	£0	£0	
VAT refunds		£0	£0	£0	
Total inflows	**£85,000**	**£49,804**	**£51,793**	**£53,899**	

Cash inflows first three months

The following image shows the cash outflows
expected over the first three months.

Cash outflows	Month 0	Month 1	Month 2	Month 3
Pasta maker machine	-£720	£0	£0	£0
Pasta makers for cookery classes (x5)	-£360	£0	£0	£0
Rolling pins (x10)	-£53	£0	£0	£0
Chopping boards (x10)	-£192	£0	£0	£0
Cutting wheels (x10)	-£64	£0	£0	£0
Accountancy, VAT & payroll		£0	£0	£0
Training courses for personnel		-£240	£0	£0
Public liability insurance		-£600	£0	£0
Employer insurance		-£600	£0	£0
Food insurance		-£600	£0	£0
Kitchen rental		-£2,074	-£2,074	-£2,074
Website & e-commerce platform		-£13	-£13	-£13
PR agency fees		-£2,400	-£2,400	-£2,400
Deliveroo subscription		-£600	£0	£0
JustEat subscription		-£354	£0	£0
Facebook ads		-£28,145	-£28,145	-£28,145
Stationery		-£10	-£10	-£10
Stamps with logo		-£60	£0	£0
Reparings		£0	£0	-£450
Card % Wix fees		-£23	-£24	-£24
Card fixed Wix fees		-£244	-£250	-£255
Direct premises rentals		£0	£0	£0
Food containers		-£460	-£488	-£517
Accessories		-£310	-£329	-£348
Packaging		-£4	-£4	-£4
Wix subscription		-£10	-£10	-£10
% commission to Deliveroo (18%)		-£4	-£4	-£5
% commission to JustEat (14%)		-£11	-£12	-£13
Perks		-£1,579	-£1,612	-£1,646
Own delivery and transport costs (variable part)		-£6,593	-£6,731	-£6,877
Refunds to customers on 20%VAT products		-£424	-£430	-£436
Refunds to customers on 0%VAT products		-£572	-£606	-£642
Ingredients		-£8,032	-£8,199	-£8,377
Ingredients online classes (12 recordings total)		-£36	£0	£0
Chef: 1 full-time		-£2,071	-£2,071	-£2,071
Direct labour cost		£0	£0	£0
Owners' remuneration		£0	£0	£0
Registration with ICO (for data protection)		-£40	£0	£0
Interest on business loan		£0	£0	£0
Other bank charges		£0	£0	£0
VAT payments		£0	£0	£0
Corporation tax (19%)		£0	£0	£0
Total cash outflows	**-£1,388**	**-£56,110**	**-£53,410**	**-£54,316**

Cash out-flows first three months

74

	Month 0	Month 1	Month 2	Month 3
Net cash flow balance (inflows - outflows)	£83,612	-£6,306	-£1,617	-£417
Operating cash balance (beginning bal. + net bal.	**£83,612**	**£77,306**	**£75,689**	**£75,272**
Additional finance requirements	£0	£0	£0	£0
Minimum desidered cash balance	£1,000	£1,000	£1,000	£1,000

The beginning balance at each month will be algebraically summed to that month's cash inflows and outflows so you will end up with a new final cash balance, better called "operating cash balance". The latter will then be carried forward on to the following month so the exercise can be repeated over again up to month 12.

The main point of cash flows projections is to show that at the end of each month you (realistically) expect to end up with a positive operating balance, this having the ultimate purpose of demonstrating that the funding requested will be sufficient for you to run your operations without needing any more financing.

In my business plans, I also include a line called "Additional finance required" and another line called "Minimum desired cash balance" (in this example being at £1,000). The purpose here is to show the reader that the business wants to have a balance of at least £1,000 at each month and that, according to your cash flow projections, the operating balance will never fall below that.

On the next page is a set of three-year cash flow projections including both forecast inflows and outflows.

Cash flows projections	Year 1	Year 2	Year 3
Beginning balance	£0	£214,003	£409,834
Cash inflows	**Year 1**	**Year 2**	**Year 3**
Ready-to-eat dishes (+VAT 20%)	£63,862	£77,912	£84,145
Cook-at-home (VAT 0%)	£482,145	£588,216	£635,274
Sales classes (+VAT 20%)	£212,587	£221,091	£226,618
Owners' funding	£5,000	£0	£0
External funding	£80,000	£0	£0
VAT refunds	£30,416	£38,696	£39,026
Total inflows	**£874,010**	**£925,915**	**£985,063**
Cash outflows	**Year 1**	**Year 2**	**Year 3**
Investments (+VAT 20%)	-£1,388	£0	£0
Operating 20%VAT expenses (+VAT 20%)	-£508,529	-£527,257	-£538,681
Ingredients, wages, rates & other non-VAT expenses	-£134,918	-£158,854	-£169,500
Refunds to customers on 20%VAT products	-£5,529	-£5,980	-£6,215
Refunds to customers on 0%VAT products	-£9,643	-£11,764	-£12,705
Corporation tax (previous year)	£0	-£26,229	-£42,212
VAT payments	£0	£0	£0
Total outflows	**-£660,007**	**-£730,085**	**-£769,314**
Net cash flow balance (inflows - outflows)	£214,003	£195,831	£215,749
Operating cash balance (beginning bal. + net bal.	**£214,003**	**£409,834**	**£625,583**
Additional finance requirements	£0	£0	£0
Minimum desidered cash balance	£1,000	£1,000	£1,000

ROI AND OTHER IMPORTANT

FINANCIAL RATIOS

ROI: net profits / investments. We often see the acronym ROI (Return on Investment). It is in the form of a percentage and, as the term suggests, shows the yearly rate at which your investments are expected to be profitable giving you an idea of their pay-back time.

What should a ROI be for an investment to be considered profitable? It depends on the sector and on many other circumstances but, as a general rule, if the ROI is too low it means the pay-back time is too long and the investment may not be worth it. Vice versa, a high ROI anticipates an interesting investment.

Debt to equity: liabilities / equity. It indicates the level of debt in relation to the amount put in by the founders/investors as equity (share capital in a company). Such metric will be used by investors and lenders alike to assess if you are borrowing too much compared to your business capabilities.

Quick ratio or acid test: (current assets – inventory) / current liabilities. This index shows how current liabilities are covered by current assets (short-term credits and cash). Ideally, you will want a situation where short-term debts are not high compared to your short-term assets.

Working capital or current ratio: current assets / current liabilities. This index also helps understand how short-term debts are covered by your business' current assets.

Sales growth: sales variation / sales previous period. Many factors can come into play here, including the general economy, the political stability of the country, the upcoming competition, how happy customers will be, and more, so a prudential approach should always be taken. You should never forecast over-optimistic figures as it would show the business plan is not reliable.

Gross profit margin: gross profit / net sales, whereas the gross profit is obtained by subtracting the costs of the goods sold from the net revenue and the net revenue are the sales less any returns of products.

Operating profit margin: operating profit / net sales, with the operating profit being the gross profit deducted of the operating expenses which are not part of the costs of goods sold.

Earnings per share: estimate net profit / number of shares offered. This is another important metric that any investor will look at to determine how much their earnings could be compared to the funds they are asked to contribute.

The above are just some of the ratios used to assess the viability of a business idea. More ratios may be included if they can help the reader understand your business profitability.

WRITING A REALISTIC BUSINESS PLAN

You must have watched Dragons' Den at least once. If you have, you will have noticed how many times contestants did a great job at presenting their idea but then, when asked about financials, they responded starry-eyed with crazy figures. From that moment they would get either laughed at or chewed out.

Nothing too surprising if the entrepreneur has not carried out a realistic examination of their forecasts and their plan.

In all fairness, anything can be in life. An idea might turn out to be the next game-changer, but the thing is it will take time before this happens.

A wise investor will certainly welcome a proposition based on realistic projections and will take you more seriously. And this is already a good enough reason to make sure you check against the reality of things, analyse your industry statistics, and make a critical analysis of your own figures, possibly reviewing them with an expert.

We know that for a new business to enter a market, a lot of marketing, promotion and dedication are necessary.

In any market are barriers to entry. And even if the product/service is a complete game-changer, it will take months to get known and get your prospects to understand the value of your proposition.

Strategic, proactive, realistic. These are the three words I would say to anyone looking to embark on a new business venture.

Do your part, analyse your whole idea and then, once you are happy with the result, put down a great business plan!

Show investors and all stakeholders, that you know what you are doing.

Show them your proposition is strong and you want to get somewhere.

Show them you mean business!

Thank you for reading my book

ABOUT THE AUTHOR

Alessandro is a business and compliance consultant with a passion for giving real added value to new and existing businesses. Over the years, he has helped entrepreneurs blueprint their path to success giving each one of  them the made-to-measure support they needed.

Since his degree in Economics and Business, he has accrued remarkable experience working with entrepreneurs and with professional firms where he was in charge for taking care of many companies in the UK.

Alessandro lives in south London, where he runs his consultancy Bolasco Consulting. With an innate love for creating and writing, Alessandro decided to create a guidance book that provide concrete help to small start-ups.

More about Alessandro can be found on his consultancy's website:

www.bolasco-consulting.com